A book for the Muslim woman

المقارنة بين الحجاب والسفور

A comparison between

VEILING
AND
UNVEILING

By:

Halah Bint Abdullah

Introducion by:
Sheikh Abdullah Ahmad Al-Swailem

DARUSSALAM
GLOBAL LEADER IN ISLAMIC BOOKS
Riyadh • Jeddah • Sharjah • Lahore
London • Houston • New York

CONTENTS

Contents

Preface

All praise be to Allah, the Lord of the Lords. Thanks to the success granted by Allah as good deeds can be achieved by His Will only. May peace and blessings be upon Muhammad, the most noblest Prophet who imparted (disclosed) the revealed Message and admonished his nation by delivering the truth honestly. Peace may also be upon those who follow his path until the Day of Judgement.

Allah says in the Qur'ân

﴿ يَٰٓأَيُّهَا ٱلَّذِينَ ءَامَنُواْ ٱتَّقُواْ ٱللَّهَ حَقَّ تُقَاتِهِۦ وَلَا تَمُوتُنَّ إِلَّا وَأَنتُم مُّسْلِمُونَ ﴾

"O you who believe! Fear Allah (by doing all that He has ordered and abstaining from all that He has forbidden) as He should be feared. [Obey Him, be thankful to Him, and remember Him (always)], and die not except in a state of Islam (as Muslims) with complete submission to Allah." (3:102)

﴿ وَٱلْمُؤْمِنُونَ وَٱلْمُؤْمِنَٰتُ بَعْضُهُمْ أَوْلِيَآءُ بَعْضٍ يَأْمُرُونَ بِٱلْمَعْرُوفِ وَيَنْهَوْنَ عَنِ ٱلْمُنكَرِ وَيُقِيمُونَ ٱلصَّلَوٰةَ وَيُؤْتُونَ ٱلزَّكَوٰةَ وَيُطِيعُونَ ٱللَّهَ وَرَسُولَهُۥٓ أُوْلَٰٓئِكَ سَيَرْحَمُهُمُ ٱللَّهُ إِنَّ ٱللَّهَ عَزِيزٌ حَكِيمٌ ﴾

"The believers, men and women, are 'Auliyâ' (helpers, supporters, friends, protectors) of one another, they enjoin (on the people) 'Al-Ma'rûf' (i.e., Islamic Monotheism and all what Islam orders one to do), and forbid (people) from 'Al-Munkar' (i.e., polytheism and disbelief of all kinds, and all what Islam has forbidden); they offer their prayers perfectly (Iqamat-as-Salat); and give the Zakat (obligatory charity) and obey Allah and His Messenger. Allah will have His Mercy on them. Surely Allah is Almighty, All-Wise." (9:71)

The truest speech is the Holy Book of Allah, and the best guidance is that of Muhammad ﷺ and the worst actions are those cheated, fabricated and woven by man. These will be counted as heresy and each heresy is an offense whose doer will be in Hell-fire.

With this view, I present to you — my Muslim sisters — these comparative norms between the veiled and unveiled woman (virtue and vice) or rather between right and wrong. It is the right which one should adhere with as the Prophet ﷺ says: "I have left to you the Book of Allah and my Sunnah (traditions), if you hold fast to them, you will never mislead."

Hence, any misleading tenet conflicting with the ordinances of Allah, His Prophet ﷺ and the limits nominated by Islamic jurisprudence shall at all times remain detested and called as abominated vices (sins).

Allah says in the Qu'rân:

﴿ وَمَن يُشَاقِقِ ٱلرَّسُولَ مِنۢ بَعْدِ مَا تَبَيَّنَ لَهُ ٱلْهُدَىٰ وَيَتَّبِعْ غَيْرَ سَبِيلِ ٱلْمُؤْمِنِينَ نُوَلِّهِۦ مَا تَوَلَّىٰ وَنُصْلِهِۦ جَهَنَّمَ وَسَآءَتْ مَصِيرًا ﴾

"And whoever contradicts and opposes the Messenger (Muhammad ﷺ) after the right path has been shown clearly to him, and follows other than the believers way. We shall keep him in the path he has chosen, and burn him in Hell — what an evil destination." (4:115)

Introduction

All praise be to Allah, He Who created us from a single person, created on a like nature, his mate and from them twain, scattered countless men and women.

I praise Allah with such a praise which compatibles with His Greatness and His Ultimate Sovereignty, and I further certify that there is no god worthy to be worshipped but Allah and that Muhammad is His last Messenger.

The women have received all attention from Islam. Allah has revealed unto His Prophet, Muhammad ﷺ in the Qu'rân some Verses dealing specially with the women. Furthermore, there is a Surah in the Qur'ân named "The Women", and Allah has made clear in His Book and through His Messenger the specific rules relevant to the women and also showed up the principles which save her from the darkness of ignorance and from the abominated ways of the people of pleasure, whims (caprice) and sex.

According to Islam, a woman is the mother, wife, sister and a daughter who has rights to take and duties to serve.

He is the Prophet ﷺ who recommended to the nation so as to preserve and take care of her. This was during the performance of the last and farewell Haj.

A woman is the source of happiness to her husband and the tender (loving) mother to her children. Therefore, Allah ordered her to cover her whole body and to stay in her home. It is the home inside which she can give ultimate tenderness, love and kindness because it is the natural place where she can exercise such qualities. Allah says in Qur'ân:

﴿وَقَرْنَ فِي بُيُوتِكُنَّ﴾

"And stay quietly in your houses" (Al-Ahzab : 33)

Islam ordained her to draw her veil over her bosom and not to display her beauty and to cast her outer garment over her (when abroad) that is most convenient that she should be known.

﴿يَٰٓأَيُّهَا ٱلنَّبِيُّ قُل لِّأَزْوَٰجِكَ وَبَنَاتِكَ وَنِسَآءِ ٱلْمُؤْمِنِينَ يُدْنِينَ عَلَيْهِنَّ مِن جَلَٰبِيبِهِنَّ ذَٰلِكَ أَدْنَىٰٓ أَن يُعْرَفْنَ﴾

"O Prophet! Tell your wives and your daughters and the women of the believers to draw their cloaks (veils) all over their bodies. That will be better, that they should be known so as not to be annoyed. (Al-Ahzab:59)

When the opponents of Islam realized this prestige of respect, reverence and eminence which the Muslim woman enjoys, they envied her for this status. Accordingly, they started plotting against her and watched for her disaster by setting traps everywhere. Moreover, they introduced several toxic movements such as Emancipation Movement, Equilibrium Movement and Captivation or Temptation Movement in which they showed peace and mercy for them and wrath, disaster and punishment for the women outside these movements. Every effort is being made to undermine values, morales and to expose the sexual affairs publicly and openly using latest models and modes of display and exhibition. Hence, the biggest desire or attention of the woman focussed on adopting and having naked (seducing) dresses. She came out to the streets and started working outside the home in company with men using her dirtiest weapons of allurement. The Muslim woman learnt the tactics of enchantment by watching the lewd films, licentious photos and reading the sexual novels. Readily, she can find the male and female guides from among those in her environment who speak her own language to explain her the way by which she can be attractive (charming) whether at home or in the street, both on optical and acoustical levels through being complaisant in speech, motions, clothing, make up (cosmetics), walking, sitting and even in looks. Such notions, unfortunately, decayed the pudency of the Muslim woman. Thus, she carried on paying no heed in going out naked, displaying her charms to anybody who likes thereof and thereby leading to the stirring up of man's sexual (animal) appeal. Conversely, if she adhered by to the covering of her whole body (wearing the Islamic lawful veil), they will consider her a retrograde and backward (retarded) woman. At this point resistance from her would vanish and replaced by submissiveness.

Muhammad Qutub, the well-known scholar رحمه الله تعالى has stated the following incidence:

Years ago, a scene on the seaside took place. There was a lady who was still keeping a little bit of shyness (the innate natural shyness of the female) after she wore the sea-dress.

He writes: This lady had the 'swimming suit' on and sat on the sand around the beach and let the cameraman have a photo for her.

He wonders what had happened as he reiterated writing: The lady sat, because of a little remainder of pudency, in a position of drawing her legs together.

The cameraman, however went to space (widen) her two legs to get the photo in modern style; but she having in her little amount of shyness refused to do so. Then, he exclaimed and persuaded her by an accent bearing the meaning of Allah! and continued; "Are you a farmer (for being conservative) or what .... ?" Immediately in a moment his words crept into her heart and spoiled the last remnant of shyness; and therefore she responded and resat with her legs opened wide in a savage (barbaric) relaxedness.

This story portrates the plans of enemies of Islam against the Muslim ladies, but Allah will complete His Light, even though the unbelievers may detest.

Our ladies, therefore, have not been deceived by these destructive ideologies, on the contrary they viewed these with mockery, and with eyes of might and pride for their religion and its teachings, the matter for which Allah is deserved to be praised and favoured as He safeguarded them with their veils and screened (covered) them.

Some pious ladies rose to instruct those women (in a few number) who deviated from the right path; and by Allah's Will they are on the way back to the straight path and adherence to the Islamic approach.

On top of those pious advisors who are giving advice to the ladies of the nation is our sister Hala, the daughter of Abdullah, who wrote this treatise which is small in volume, but big in meaning and contents. This treatise is like an ambush in our hands, armoured with juristic evidences, alive sayings and valuable pieces of advice to make the inviters of error stumble and tear them into pieces.

May Allah Almighty bless our Islamic sister for her sincere effort and reward her for the guidance she provided to her fellow sisters. In the last, we should always say: Praise be to Allah, the Cherisher and Sustainer of the worlds; and may peace and blessings be upon our Prophet, Muhammad ﷺ, the last of the Messengers.

Abdullah Ahmed Al-Swailam
Imam of Al-Shahail Villages Mosque

ISLAM IS A GIFT OF ALLAH TO HUMANITY

My sister in Islam : Allah تعال,Glory be to Him, has bestowed us with the blessings of Islam and Belief (Faith) together with their inclusive (latent) might and pride for the whole humanity generally, and the woman in particular. Islam has honoured her so much. It has laid down the legitimate laws which protect her chastity and also secure for her the ways of self-realization, dignity and the fulfilment of her rights. Thus, the Muslim woman has been featured by matchless privileges which has raised her prestige and standing thereby enabling her to hail and get pride of being the women who is overwhelmed with sobriety, reverence, respect and lofty honour.

Such qualities are so high and exalted that they cannot be reached to; and are so noble that they cannot be touched by the hands of the frivolous (wicked), or even viewed by the eyes of the licentious. Hereunder, we pinpoint some of the trans-phrased poetry verses said by a veiled lady, boasting of her veil:

With the hand of chastity I protect the glory of my veil, and by my infallibility (purity) I over-run (precede) my peers.

Armoured with my witty intellect and far-sighted innate disposition (faculty), I complete my morals (decency).

My best education and ethics never cause me any harm because I'm full in my mind and have the ability to judge the situations.

Also, I'm not in a position of being hindered to embark the summit. This is because I covered my whole body and don't expose my beauty publicly.

As can clearly be seen, we quite admit that the prescription of wearing the veil for woman is the greatest precaution for her. This is because the veil is the stronghold to each woman since it cautions her against harm and the influence of the one in whose heart is a disease.

Veil is lawfully (legitimately) defined as the dress which should cover (veil) the whole body of the woman including the hands, face and feet. It is a must that it should be with a loose and wide garment which neither materialize or increase the body in volume nor show her qualities.

Veil has been prescribed legitimately upon women to block out the occurrence of the temptation between man and woman.

Allah (glory be to Him) said in His Holy Book,

﴿ يَٰٓأَيُّهَا ٱلنَّبِيُّ قُل لِّأَزْوَٰجِكَ وَبَنَاتِكَ وَنِسَآءِ ٱلْمُؤْمِنِينَ يُدْنِينَ عَلَيْهِنَّ مِن جَلَٰبِيبِهِنَّ ذَٰلِكَ أَدْنَىٰٓ أَن يُعْرَفْنَ فَلَا يُؤْذَيْنَ ﴾

"O Prophet! Tell your wives and your daughters and the women of the believers to draw their cloaks (veils) all over their bodies. That will be better that they should be known so as not to be annoyed. And Allah is Ever Oft-Forgiving, Most Merciful". (33:59)

What great these Qur'ânic Verses are! .... along with their implied meanings of lofty and honourable orientations made clear to the nation in this regard. We notice among the measures taken in this respect that Allah commands His Prophet ﷺ to enjoin his wives, the mothers of believers and his daughters, may Allah accept them all and obligate the women of believers to the wearing of the veil. This is in order to retain and develop their dignity safe from becoming the subject of vicious rumours.

EVIDENCE FOR THE VEIL FROM THE TRADITIONS (SUNNAH)

Allah may shower His Mercy on the Women of Al-Ansaar who on hearing the revelation of Allah that they should "Draw their cloaks (veils) all over their bodies" and '(when abroad) they go out motionless or silent with awe as a result of being in tranquility (to appear as if they have put crows on their heads) and they should have black garments on them'.

The Holy Qur'ân states:

$$\text{وَإِذَا سَأَلْتُمُوهُنَّ مَتَعًا فَسْتَلُوهُنَّ مِن وَرَاءِ حِجَابٍ ذَلِكُمْ أَطْهَرُ لِقُلُوبِكُمْ وَقُلُوبِهِنَّ}$$

"And when you ask (Prophet's wives) for anything you want, ask them from behind a screen, that is purer for your hearts and for their hearts." (33:53)

The reason is that the veil (Al-Hijab) is a purity (cleanliness) for the hearts of the believing men and women. It is also a strong and purified tool or shield for the hearts against deviation or inclination towards the prohibited desire; a safer condition which prevents falling into trial; much more protection for observing the chastity of both man and woman;

acting as a barrier between them and vice and keeping them far away from committing sins (disobedience) or even thinking thereof. Hence, Allah, the All-Omnipotent, the All-Sublime has presented and put the woman through these revered Verses in a high position with a paramount consideration similar to that of the valuable gem, or rather being more precious than the priceless gem. According to the Islamic jurisprudence, she is the created being for giving the chaste births and a source of virtue and honour. She will always be endowed by this rank, only when she keeps abiding by the ethics of Islam and its eminent teachings.

This has been clearly illustrated in the benevolent Qur'ânic Verses revealed for the sake of the chaste, pure and devout mothers of the believers. Such Verses were also for the women of the believing men who submitted to the ordinances of Allah تعالى ,Glory be to Him, and acted accordingly to the best and proper way. We supplicate Allah to accept the mothers of the believers, and He may recompensate them generously for being in a state of guidance and being the favoured role models and the optimum exemplar for the whole Muslim ladies. They had the precedence of following the Light of Allah and His Messenger ﷺ besides being fully educated with the rules of conduct of Allah and His Messenger. This prompted them to apply the laws of Islam along with its teachings in the system Allah ordained for them, and in the form the Prophet liked.

THE CONDITIONS OF THE LEGAL (LEGITIMATE) VEIL

My sister in Islam: We draw the attention that the permissible veil (Al-Hijab Ay-Shariy) should have certain characteristics and conditions through which the Muslim woman can be specified (recognized) from among others. The best form for the veil is the garment (cloak) which should cover the whole body of the woman starting from the head down to the toes of her feet. Allah states in the Qur'ân that they should: ﴿يُدْنِينَ عَلَيْهِنَّ مِن جَلَٰبِيبِهِنَّ﴾

"Draw their cloaks (veils) all over their bodies (when abroad)". (33:59)

Allah also says: ﴿وَلْيَضْرِبْنَ بِخُمُرِهِنَّ عَلَىٰ جُيُوبِهِنَّ﴾

"And to draw their veils over their bosoms" (24:31).

Further, Allah addressed only to the believing women to wear the veil by His Saying, "And say to the believing woman", as well as His Saying in the Verse, "And the believing women".

From the point of view of Hadith, it was mentioned (narrated) that: Some women came to see Aiysha رضي الله عنها, (they entered Aiysha's room) while they had fine dresses on. However, Aiysha said:, "If you were believing women, then such would not be the suitable dress of the believing women, but if you were not, you can enjoy wearing it."

From the above foregoing, the lawful veil is the one which screens the whole body including the face and palms of the hands — such is not the veil through which a woman displays her charms by covering the head only while exposing her body and the face. We come to the conclusion that any dress whatsoever which covers the body including the head, exposing however, the complexion of the woman or increasing her body in volume or showing her charms to any body staring at her, would be deemed to be illicit because it makes the woman play her enchantment, and so it will contradict with the warning of Allah to man against the allurement of the Satan (devil) regarding the subject of clothing (dress). This meaning is depicted clearly in the following Qur'ânic Verses:

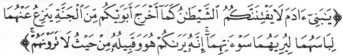

"O Children of Adam! Let not Satan deceive you, as he got your parents (Adam and Eve) out of Paradise, stripping them of their raiments, to show them their private parts. Verily, he and his tribe see you from a position where you cannot see them." (7:27)

Allah also says in the Qur'ân:

﴿ يَبَنِيٓ ءَادَمَ قَدۡ أَنزَلۡنَا عَلَيۡكُمۡ لِبَاسًا يُوَٰرِى سَوۡءَٰتِكُمۡ وَرِيشًا وَلِبَاسُ ٱلتَّقۡوَىٰ ذَٰلِكَ خَيۡرٌ ذَٰلِكَ مِنۡ ءَايَٰتِ ٱللَّهِ لَعَلَّهُمۡ يَذَّكَّرُونَ ﴾

"O Children of Adam! We have bestowed raiment upon you to cover yourselves (screen your private parts etc.) and as an adornment. But the raiment of righteousness that is better. Such are among the Ayât (proofs, evidences, verses, lessons, signs, revelations, etc.) of Allah, that they may remember (i.e., leave the falsehood and follow the Truth). (7:26)

Furthermore, Allah - The Almighty has warned man in several Qur'ânic Verses and by the sayings of His prophets and Messengers against inciting of the damned Satan who by fraud and deceit succeeded in getting Adam and his wife out of the Paradise as well as stripping them off their raiments (dresses).

Now Satan is doing the same that he did to our

forefather Adam, he is striving hard to persuade Adam's progeny, bidding them indecency, impeding them to behave according to the laws regulated by Allah and alluring mischief to them.

For this, and to avoid such devious actions, Allah legitimated the laws and made known to mankind the dress which hides the beauty and finery of woman; protects her dignity and safeguards her against the evils of error and the malicious incentives.

It suffices man that Allah has revealed the Qur'ân which is a healing and a mercy for him and which keeps (preserves) his dignity and rights. He confers on man the right precepts to which if he adheres will never go astray, and made clear to men what harms them and what benefits them. To this limit of the rationale, we come to the following conditions upon which the legitimate (legal) veil should conform with:

First: The veil should cover the whole body of the woman including the face and palms of the hands, besides being fully beauty and finery proof (concealing).

Second: The covering must not be decorated or embellished with various colours but it should be of opaque material with only one colour so as not to be attractive or draw the attentions to.

Third: The covering should be opaque and loose and not to be translucent that reveals the woman's shape or what she is wearing underneath it.

Fourth: It should not be designed in simulation to the clothing of the non-believing women from the aspects of the new modes and fashions. This requires that shape and appearance of the covering should be ordinary and familiar.

Fifth: It should not be similar to manly fashions as regards to colour and design because Prophet Muhammad ﷺ is reported as having said that: «لَعَنَ اللهُ المُتَشَبِّهِيْنَ مِنَ الرِّجَالِ بِالنِّسَاءِ وَالمُتَشَبِّهَاتِ مِنَ النِّسَاءِ بِالرِّجَالِ»

"Allah condemns those men who behave or act in a woman like fashion, and those women who behave or act in a man like fashion".

Sixth: The covering should be somewhat cheap and not so much costly which reflects the character of extravagancy, squandering and wasting of money — the fact which leads the woman to fall in hypocrisy and the eager desire for seeking reputation or fame. The Prophet ﷺ says: "He who likes to be overwhelmed with reputation, Allah will reveal and make people know about his untrue intention, and he who acts ostentatiously, Allah will also make a show of his unaccepted behaviour (divulge his hiding aims).

Seventh: The covering should not have even a small amount of perfume nor it be slightly censed because it is not permissible for the Muslim woman to get perfumed and get out of her home.

The Prophet was reported to have said,

«كُلُّ عَيْنٍ زَانِيَةٌ وَالْمَرْأَةُ إِذَا اسْتَعْطَرَتْ فَمَرَّتْ بِالْمَجْلِسِ فَهِيَ كَذَا»

"Every eye is adulterous and when a woman perfumes herself and passes a company, she is such and such (meaning adulterous)".
(Collected by At-Tirmidhee and Abu Dawood).

UNCOVERING (OF THE FACE) IS A HERETICAL DEED WITH UNDERLYING DISMERITS

Unveiling is a heresy, error and a violation of both the Islamic religion and the purified tradition (Sunnah). It is an evidence that a woman who uncovers has a weakness in belief as it strips her from chastity and modesty, taking in consideration that these two qualities (features) are from the branches of Faith (Belief). Additionally, uncovering takes away dignity and the granted legal rights from the woman, revealing of her private parts, exposing her shortcomings (faults) and spoiling (wasting) her feminity. It represents an adherent character for the woman who has already stripped off modesty and chastity, contrary to those who are complied with the ordinances of Allah and the significance lying behind.

Hereunder we mention some of the disadvantages of uncovering (the face or any part of the body):

First: A woman being unveiled will be in a state of rebellion against Islamic society and disobedience of the precepts of Allah — the Omnipotent — Who created her.

Second: She will be violating the legitimate rules of her true Islamic religion, as well as the purified laws of the Prophet's traditions (Sunnah).

Third: Such woman will be breaching the honoured morals of Islam giving no heed thereto in case of being unveiled.

Fourth: Waiving the woman of her pudency and chastity which were the prime characteristics of the mothers of the believing man and women — may Allah accept them and also each believing woman.

Fifth: Uncovering will strip the woman from anything which hides (veils) her finery, charms and the genitals (private parts).

Sixth: Making the woman equal to man as to treatment and rights especially in some Islamic and Arab countries.

Seventh: Going out from home and being obliged to work in company with men.

Eighth: The unveiled woman has to follow (adopt) what the west imposes upon her of illicit notions and tenets.

Ninth: The unveiled Muslim woman will be involved in imitating the non-believing women as regards to the destructive customs and usages.

Tenth: Unveiled women would become the protectors and maintainers of men.

Eleventh: Both men and women will not be satisfied with eachother under their existing conjugal life with the mutual desire of making a new substitution.

Twelfth: The western semi-naked fashion and modes would govern and control the dress and appearance of the woman.

Thirteenth: Most male-oriented commodities are advertised by alluring naked females for attractions and promotions.

Fourteenth: Degrading and humiliating the unveiled woman in the common service and job sites which are supposed to be allocated to men only.

Fifteenth: Causing the woman to be under actions of compulsory rape and deflowering, of which incidences are seen and heard about, particularly in the advanced and civilized societies in all levels of life.

A COMPARISON BETWEEN AL-HIJAB (VEIL) AND AS-SOFUR (UNVEIL)

Allah, Almighty said in His Holy Book;

﴿ وَقَرْنَ فِى بُيُوتِكُنَّ وَلَا تَبَرَّجْنَ تَبَرُّجَ ٱلْجَٰهِلِيَّةِ ٱلْأُولَىٰ ﴾

"And stay in your houses, and do not display yourselves like that of the former times of ignorance" (33:33).

True is Allah, the Great and True is also His Prophet. All praise, appreciation and commendation be to Allah for the blessings (gifts) of Faith and Islam which He bestowed upon us. Such gifts which enhance and raise the position of the Muslim man and woman to a higher rank of honour, chastity, purity and eminence of character. Islam got them a dress which is the raiment of righteousness and belief. Through covering, Islam made them inaccessible and well fortified, averted the makers of plots from them, as well as the tease of fashion and the feelings of hatred from male violent people against them. He fixed the house to be the natural place for the woman to worship and obey Allah, considering the household jobs will be the best duty to be undertaken by the woman in the world life.

Covering is thus, by Islam, the protective screen for the woman from any evil and harm. This is contrary to man who is required by nature to work and keep performing prayers in the mosque. Moreover, man, and not the woman, is the one who has to move freely to earn living.

Glory be to You, O Allah, Exalted is Your Majesty, Great is Your Wisdom and Magnificent is Your Forgiveness and Kindness that You had mercy on the woman and made available to her the means of comfort, convenience and safety. Thanks to Allah, Who guided her to the way of deliverence from the play of bad men; evils of their malicious intentions and also the malignancy of the intentions of those who have a disease in their hearts (the prohibited inclination towards a woman). Allah kept her chastity safe against the tamper hands of the licentious people and aggressions of spoilers.

On the other hand, Allah did preserve for the woman all rights in connection with states of marriage, divorce, pregnancy, period of wait (after being divorced and husband's death), and cost of living due to her including all other things entitled to her. Allah, the Omnipotent, has referred to all these points among some Surahs and Verses of the Holy

Qur'ân, and He urged us to take care of the woman since she has been created as a weak human being, while man has been created strong, stern, resistant, and able to encounter the difficulties of life so as to earn his living.

Therefore, our generous Prophet instructed us in so many authenticated traditions to make the woman our ultimate concern. On the opposite side, he warned and drew her attention to some requirements through some other traditions which are all correct as to their chain of authorities on which a tradition is based.

In view of all these aspects — our Muslim esteemed sister — may Allah guide us and you to His Right Path. Here it is this comparison between the state of being covered and not covered, to be fully oriented and understood while reading, then only you can be convinced of the privileges of Al-Hijab (covering) along with its relevant several benefits. It is an ordinance which Allah has prescribed upon it for women, making clear at the same time the disadvantages of uncovering which is an evil suggestion from Satanic assaulting mind, an action of Satan's manoeuvres and a disowned atrocity of its abominations. May Allah give us refuge against him, for Allah hears and responds all things.

Al-Hijab (Covering): It has been prescribed upon woman by an order from Allah, Glory be to Him, which has been referred to in Qur'ân. Thus, a Muslim woman is obliged to follow, and apply the teachings of the Holy Book and Sunnah by the manner of adhering therewith, following and submitting thereto as per the laws legitimated to woman in this respect. The purpose is seeking to please Allah, the Creator, preserving both her person and her dignity.

As-Sofur (Uncovering): It is an invitation extended by Satan, foe of the Allah, and an act of his own. It is a blind imitation of those who deviated from the denominations of Islam, neither admitting it nor its lawful rules.

Hence, Muslim woman has to turn away from being unveiled and to reject it since it is a bad conduct which degrades her prestige, honour and puts down her standing, thus making her a very cheap commodity for the callers of evil and a target for the eyes of evil.

Al-Hijab (Covering): It is a sign of the completion of faith by a woman who wore it for the Fear of Allah and seeking to please Allah but not as a customary and habitual matter. The woman who covers herself will be covered with chastity, modesty and purity — and all of these qualities are the integrated part of Faith.

As-Sofur (Uncovering): It is an indicator of the weakness and shortage of the woman's Faith because it will not be limited only to the stripping of the woman from her cloak and covering, but it will also be an incentive for her to fall in the abyss of vice which will eventually lead her to become an easy access prey for any criminal, cheating and perverted man. The fact that her virginity can be deflowered, her chastity could be polluted, and finally be left alone in the worst condition as a most regrettable exemplar never known before.

Al-Hijab (Covering): It is a screen for the woman, as woman's whole body, from the top of her head to the tip of the toe, is deemed to be private parts (not to be seen). Nevertheless, Allah raised the woman to a higher rank, preserved her honour and purity and took her away from the tiring paths and disgrace. He prevents any man, who could possibly marry, to see her (excluding those who could not). Since, as mentioned previously, women are advised not to make a public display of their beauty in the sense that they are obliged to cover all their bodies including charms and weaknesses (shortcomings). Thus, a woman is going to veil what is beautiful and ugly of her own, by the fact that nobody will be able to see her; her dignity, feelings, and womanliness remain safe and also her rights as a human being will not be oppressed spiritually or corporeally.

As-Sofur (Uncovering): It strips a woman from anything which is thought to be viewed as a semi-naked person free from reverence, solemnity and appropriate to the biased looks of diseased men, and greedy caprices which inevitably expose the charms and weaknesses of her corporality. Such a woman enshrouded with such circumstances would make her feeble and involved in dead locks that prevent her from happy and honourable life.

Al-Hijab (Covering): It is a crown over every pious Muslim woman who has a common sense for what benefits her, what harms her and what hurts her dignity and feelings. Such a conservative woman will be like twinkling pearls preserved away from the hands of wicked and curious persons and tongues (lips) of those who play upon the woman and her rights.

As-Sofur (Uncovering): It is a placard hanged over the woman who took off the garment of modesty (pudency) and whose face has no place for any leftover shyness because it turns (becomes) to be like a picture comprising various scenes and different colours which has been disformed (disfigured) by the pens of transgressors and brushes of the cunning impudent people who used to seize one's honour. Thus she will be moved within their hands like a commodity circulated or displayed in the markets with its ugly and beautiful sides.

Here the Satanic fashion slips in between and seize the opportunity, displaying the appealing colours and all sexual chaos of females which naturally will be void of anything supposed to be chaste, hereby making her at the end like a trifle commodity or a picture on which all sorts of errors and malignancies can be tried freely. Moreover, a woman who is in the fists of such a Satanic show, would mere be a mobile tool for making illegal gains and an object for the various unrestrained actions, which will be practised in the name of emancipation, throwing behind the so called morals and good characters which every woman should be qualified with as a sign of being respectful and solemn.

Uptill now I came, my sister in Islam, to the conclusion of my comparison between Al-Hijab (covering) and As-Sofur (uncovering) — right and wrong. Only this much facts I have in my possession to say in this regard. However, if you still have, my sister, more information thereon, please don't hesitate to mention to help me and our pious Muslim sisters understand and grasp such a vital topic, which interests every Muslim lady who is fully aware to distinguish between what benefits her and what harms her; and which things increase her standing and prestige, and what decreases and degrades her significance.

It is gratifying, our Muslim sisters, to notice on this occasion some simple examples through which I will try to highlight the importance and privileges of Al-Hijab (Covering) as follows:

Example No. (1)

My Muslim sister: Suppose you have a very valuable necklace made of natural diamond or a precious jewel then you would be very keen to keep it safe and at the same time, you admire it and are fond of it. Will you go, the case as it is, and put it freely within the hands of other people or to mislocate in such a way that it can be liable to the risks of theft and loss or alternatively to keep, fear on and conserve it in a safe place where nobody's hand can be able to reach to or even to be viewed to by whatsoever eyes. Everyone around you knows that you possess a precious jewel, however, they cannot see or predict its shape or colour. Even though, they appreciate and estimate your valuable jewel highly; although they did not have any chance to see or touch it, they quite know and realize how pretty and valuable the jewel is. For being strongholded (protected) by something similar to Al-Hijab (Covering), such shield make them think thousand times before their hands try to reach to. Such a perfect jewel of splendid qualities and being fully conserved in like the Muslim veiled woman, who in herself, is considered to be a valuable jewel whose value is increased by this protected veil which keeps her away from any hurt or harm.

This point is amply illustrated in the following Verses of the Qur'ân:

$$﴿ ذَٰلِكَ أَدْنَىٰ أَن يُعْرَفْنَ فَلَا يُؤْذَيْنَ ﴾$$

"That will be better, that they should be known (as free respectable women) so as not to be annoyed." (33:59)

Example No. (2)

Let it be imagined that you, my Muslim sister, are standing amid the border which separates two pretty (nice) cities, both of which attract the passers-by. One of the two cities has a big and very high surrounding fence which encircles entirely the whole city in the form that it becomes invisible.

The other city, on the other hand, has no fort and bared of any protective fence (wall) to border it, as well as its milestone. Thus, it is visible to everyone that anyone who passes by can see and enjoy its beauty. They may enter and take away some of or all its resources (treasures) and hurt its firm stance. Hence, it would become as an open city or unrestricted bridge or path which can easily be crossed and reviewed by all people. Such city for being not protected by a fort or a fence encourages people to attack it, taking whatever cheap and expensive, paying no attention to any penalty or punishment.

So, this open city got used to give freely, not to take; to grow, not to harvest; and to produce, not to pick the fruits thereof.

For being not conservative, it gives everything to the extent that even its own rights are wasted away. Consequently, this city would be deserted, scorned and neglected. It would also become barren and bared of any sort of good things (advantages) thereon because it permitted for itself to open its gates widely to receive everybody and his brother, moreover, allowing them to get acquainted with its hiding secrets and beauty, hereby giving them the chance to play and spoil it to the moment they stripped it of what precious and valuable is. The only thing the city gathered therefrom is regret and sorrow.

As regards to the other conservative pretty city along with its underlying blessings, welfares and concealing charms, all in all will be kept safe-guarded due to Allah's Protection. Firstly and lastly to the fort with the fence circling it from all parts and sides, thus preventing the curious people who desire to attack it or to have mere a look thereon.

The task of such a formidable fort confined not only in preventing (hindering) those evil people to enter it, but it also added to this city, a highly reverred and lofty eminence so that nobody can attack it for he knows that around this huge fenced fort there is a magnificent city which comprises so many blessings. He, however, cannot and never dare to attack it. By this way, the city can defend its entity, its reputation and what Allah bestowed upon of blessings, dignity and honour providing such things for itself first, natives (inhabitants) and those enjoying the very high positions therein, heeding no care about what the people of weak spirits and hearts of disease (grudge) say or spread of fictitious lies and bad rumours against it. Those evil people when they fail to get what they want, start scattering bad rumours doing their best to stick to accusations thereof, to make an interesting speech material for rumouring and the subject of their spoiling and tendentious pens.

Now, my sister in Islam, after you have read these examples, you came to the conclusion that anything which is formidably strongholded can never be hurt or exploited badly.

The other side of the coin is the thing which is manifestly evident to everybody, a fact which finally will come to a damaged and destructive end, keeping in mind that the Muslim believing woman is, however, not in a position to make equal or similar to anything whatsoever, because she is more precious and valuable than the jewel itself or anything else to be resembled with. This is clearly brought to light in Surah of Saffat (Those Ranged in Ranks), where Allah resembles the women of Paradise as: "(Delicate and pure) as if they were (hidden) eggs (well) preserved" (37:49), and in Surah of Waqi'a (the Inevitable Event) as: "Like unto preserved pearls." (56:43). Allah, glory be to Him, is the All-Omnipotent, the All-Great, Who Himself has appreciated and dignified the question of the Muslim woman, and given her full care.

Allah, the Transcendent, is the Creator, the Evolver and the Bestower of forms, Who has His Own Ultimate Wisdom and Example (lesson) lying behind the concept of woman which is neither grasped by minds, nor comprehended by selves

Allah - The Absolute - is the Most Cautious of His creatures than anybody else. Therefore, He has given them the Judgement by which they can choose the right and the difficult way. Allah says in the Qur'ân, "And shown him the two ways (good and evil)". (90:10).

It rests to present these pieces of advice to every Muslim believing woman who is earnestly concerned with her religion and her person:

1. Covering, my sister in Islam, is the tradition of you, and those who preceded you. It is lawfully incumbent upon you by Islam. The mothers of the believing men namely the spouses of the Prophet ﷺ , and his esteemed daughters (رضي الله عنهن) and the believing women have abided by covering the face and the whole body before you all through the centuries and times.

2. I'm still addressing my speech to you, my sister in

Islam, saying that she, who keeps wearing the veil (Al-Hijab) decreed for her by Allah and decided by the tradition (Sunnah) of His Prophet Muhammad ﷺ will be served as her own protective shield and the weapon with which she can defend herself against the foes of Islam.

3. Covering, my Muslim sister, is your weapon which you should bear in all spheres at anytime and everywhere you go to. It frightens anyone who dares to look at you while you are wearing it. For this, take it as your permanent weapon against wars proclaimed by enemies of Islam on the Muslim woman.

4. You should have to consider, my sister in Islam, covering as an argument, not against you but for you, by which you can confute (or argue) with anyone to be ignorant, outrage or oppressor, to hold their tongues and gouge out their eyes.

5. It is an advice for every Muslim woman, travelling abroad, not to remove veil and uncover herself because it is the covering which raises her standing and increases her prestige and significance.

6. Be careful, my sister in Islam, not to allow

yourself involved in any attempt to imitate the unbelieving women, Jews and Christians either in the way of their modes of fashion or making a public display of their beauty and finery.

7. My sister in Islam, beware of not going after the footsteps of Satan, i.e., fashion shows.

8. My sister in Islam, don't remove away the garment of chastity and honour i.e., the cloak and covering, to substitute it by the one of shame and seduce when you go out from your own Muslim country while travelling abroad.

9. Don't try, my sister in Islam, to follow the traces of the unbelieving women as to their clothing and ways of living when you are obliged to go to their countries, and avoid taking them as your models because they never tried to imitate us when they come to our country but, on the contrary, they do their best to make us imitate them and do as they do.

10.Hence, keep in mind, my sister in Islam, to take care of their planned intentions and if you were in their countries, for certain circumstances, try to comply with wearing the cloak and covering, hereby making them perhaps to follow and imitate you and not the opposite.

11. My sister in Islam, any woman who leaves her cloak and covering feeble-mindedly, (being heedless of it) while she is extant in the country of the unbelieving men and women, they will conversely disdain and make fun of her, thereby causing her to suspect her Islamic religion.

12. Covering, my Muslim sister, is the tool which protects you against their evils, harms and notions which hurt (capture) honour and religion.

13. My sister in Islam, the foes of Islam are endeavouring and wish that they could see the Muslim woman renunciating of her good manners, morals and Islamic rules and follow them so as to have an unpleasant effect on her as they did so with (on) the women whose faith is weak.

14. My sister in Islam, be cautious that the enemies of Islam are waiting for you and others of the chaste women to meet with disaster, sparing no effort to spread their toxicity and error through the audio and visual sets so as to deviate the Muslim woman of her covering and chastity which is the only fundamental Islamic element which makes them angry, deceives them and gets their peace disturbed.

15. My sister in Islam, if you try, even for one time only, to call them to your religion or to reject their customs and traditions on whose base they have been brought up and consequently they are following them with the knowledge that all these fall into unbelief and are untrue, will they listen to you and repudiate everything behind them just for your own sake .... ? The answer will be of course negative and further to cater for such call they will be much more witty and cautious to find and invent the justifications and excuses by which they can escape easily. However, you, my sister in Islam, without being invited or given just one trial to do so, you — unfortunately — with readiness and hasty, will go to them and act as they do.

16. My sister in Islam, try seriously to be the nice symbol representing the beautiful and desirable image of Islam by calling to Islam wherever you go, being the favoured role model for your Muslim sisters, raising hereby the Word of your Lord, religion and the tradition of your Prophet Muhammad ﷺ , high over anything and throwing disappointment on the enemies of Islam, and causing their oppressing plans to fail. You have to take for yourself a resemblance of the women whose bliss will be Paradise from the part

of being chaste to become — Allah's Will — among the family of the Paradise.

In the last, I say: Praise to Allah, the Cherisher and Sustainer of the worlds, peace to all who follow guidance, and peace and blessings be upon the most honourable and noblest Prophet and Messenger, our Prophet Muhammad — peace and blessing be upon him, upon his family and all his followers.

A comparison between

VEILING
and
UNVEILING

© **Maktaba Dar-us-Salam, 2000**
King Fahd National Library Cataloging-in-Publication Data
Tharir, Abdullah Halah
Veiling and un-veiling-Riyadh.
48p., 12x17 cm. **ISBN 9960-740-54-4**
I-Veiling   II-Unveiling   III- Title
219.1 dc.   0096/16

Legal Deposit no. 0096/16
ISBN 9960-740-54-4

HEAD OFFICE

P.O. Box: 22743, Riyadh 11416 K.S.A.Tel: 00966-01-4033962/4043432 Fax: 4021659
E-mail: Riyadh@dar-us-salam.com, darussalam@awalnet.net.sa Website: www.dar-us-salam.com

K.S.A. Darussalam Showrooms:
Riyadh
Olaya branch:Tel 00966-1-4614483 Fax: 4644945
Malaz branch: Tel 4735220 Fax: 4735221
- **Jeddah**
  Tel: 00966-2-6879254 Fax: 6336270
- **Al-Khobar**
  Tel: 00966-3-8692900 Fax: 00966-3-8691551

U.A.E
- **Darussalam, Sharjah U.A.E**
  Tel: 00971-6-5632623 Fax: 5632624
  Sharjah@dar-us-salam.com

PAKISTAN
- **Darussalam,** 36 B Lower Mall, Lahore
  Tel: 0092-42-724 0024 Fax: 7354072
  Lahore@dar-us-salam.com
- Rahman Market, Ghazni Street
  Urdu Bazar Lahore
  Tel: 0092-42-7120054 Fax: 7320703

U.S.A
- **Darussalam, Houston**
  P.O Box: 79194 Tx 77229
  Tel: 001-713-722 0419 Fax: 001-713-722 0431
  E-mail: Webmaster@dar-us-salam.com
- **Darussalam, New York** 186 Atlantic Ave, Brooklyn
  New York-11217, Tel: 001-718-625 5925
  Fax: 718-625 1511
  Email: darussalamny@hotmail.com

U.K
- **Darussalam International Publications Ltd.**
  Leyton Business Centre
  Unit – 17, Etloe Road, Leyton, London, E10 7BT
  Tel: 00 44 20 8539 4885 Fax: 00 44 20 8539 4889
  Mobile: 00 44 7947 306 706
- **Darussalam International Publications Limited**
  146 Park Road,
  London NW8 7RG Tel: 00 44 20 725 2246
- **Darussalam**
  398-400 Coventry Road, Small Heath
  Birmingham, B10 0UF
  Tel: 0121 77204792 Fax: 0121 772 4345
  E-mail: info@darussalamuk.com
  Web: www.darussalamuk.com

FRANCE
- Editions & Librairie Essalam
  135, Bd de Ménilmontant- 75011 Paris
  Tél: 0033-01- 43 38 19 56/ 44 83
  Fax: 0033-01- 43 57 44 31
  E-mail: essalam@essalam.com

AUSTRALIA
- ICIS: Ground Floor 165-171, Haldon St.
  Lakemba NSW 2195, Australia
  Tel: 00612 9758 4040 Fax: 9758 4030

MALAYSIA
- E&D Books SDN. BHD.-321 B 3rd Floor,
  Suria Klcc
  Kuala Lumpur City Center 50088
  Tel: 00603-21663433
  Fax: 00603-42573758
  E-mail: endbook@tm.net.my

SINGAPORE
- Muslim Converts Association of Singapore
  32 Onan Road The Galaxy Singapore- 424484
  Tel: 0065-440 6924, 348 8344
  Fax: 440 6724

SRI LANKA
- Darul Kitab 6, Nimal Road, Colombo-4
  Tel: 0094-1-589 038 Fax: 0094-74 722433

KUWAIT
- Islam Presentation Committee
  Enlightment Book Shop
  P.O. Box: 1613, Safat 13017 Kuwait
  Tel: 00965-244 7526, Fax: 240 0057

INDIA
- Islamic Dimensions
  56/58 Tandel Street (North)
  Dongri, Mumbai 4000 009,India
  Tel: 0091-22-3736875, Fax: 3730689
  E-mail:sales@IRF.net

SOUTH AFRICA
- Islamic Da'wah Movement (IDM)
  48009 Qualbert 4078 Durban,South Africa
  Tel: 0027-31-304-6883
  Fax: 0027-31-305-1292
  E-mail: idm@ion.co.za